Words of Praise for **Being There**

"It is indeed a beautiful book of p[...]
It portrays not only a deep spiritua[...] [...]s
to reflect upon the Rosary."

-Most Reverend Gregory M. Aymond,
Archbishop of New Orleans.

"The crystal clarity and love evident in every word of Marie
Louise Nix's poetry in *Being There* takes me to a refreshing, deep
level of prayer and meditation. This book is simply beautiful;
It will touch your heart and mind."

-Pamela Binnings Ewen, author of
Faith on Trial and *The Secret of the Shroud,*
President, Northshore Literary Society and
Board Member of the Tennessee Williams Literary Festival

And on other works by Marie Louise Nix

Commenting on another work by Marie Louise Nix, the
internationally acclaimed Catholic novelist and philosopher Walker
Percy wrote: (Marie Louise's writing) has very special qualities... an
unapologetic, non-polemical Catholicism, which is quite unique and
quite appealing." Appointed by Pope John Paul II to the Pontifical
Commission on the Arts, Mr. Percy was the recipient of the National
Book Award, The Laetare Medal, the Jefferson Lecture in the
Humanities and many other awards.

"Beautiful and profound work.... Truly anointed of God."
-Judy Klein, Professor of Theology, Holy Cross College

"Brings the reader to new dimensions of spirituality."
-Elizabeth Moore, author, and Times Picayune columnist

"An outpouring of grace. An enormous talent."
-Karen Edmunds, New Orleans artist
MFA University of Vermont

Also by Marie Louise Guste Nix

Visions of Splendor: Poems and Images of the Beyond in our Midst

Transportation to the Higher Place: Poems of the Way

Restoring Soul: Poems of Healing, Encounter,
Awareness, and Empowerment

BEING THERE

Reflections from the Scenes of the
Mysteries of the Rosary

MARIE LOUISE GUSTE NIX

WESTBOW
PRESS
A DIVISION OF THOMAS NELSON
& ZONDERVAN

★ [Scripture quotations are from] Revised Standard Version of the Bible—Second Catholic Edition (Ignatius Edition) Copyright © 2006 National Council of the Churches of Christ in the United States of America. Used by permission. All rights reserved.

WestBow Press books may be ordered through booksellers or by contacting:

WestBow Press
A Division of Thomas Nelson & Zondervan
1663 Liberty Drive
Bloomington, IN 47403
www.westbowpress.com
1 (866) 928-1240

ISBN: 978-1-4908-1984-6 (sc)
ISBN: 978-1-4908-1983-9 (e)

Library of Congress Control Number: 2013922864

Printed in the United States of America.

WestBow Press rev. date: 3/7/2014

CONTENTS

Dedication

To my Mother and Father

Dorothy Schutten Guste and William J. Guste, Jr

*Who blessed our home life with devotion to the Blessed Mother
and the daily recitation of the Blessed Mother's Rosary*

ACKNOWLEDGEMENTS

First and foremost, it is due to a patient and merciful God that I have been able to produce this work, proving that "anything is possible with God."

My parents lived the evangelical virtues in a buoyant and fun environment. They brought an abundance of joy into the family situation so that God didn't seem synonymous with judgment or pious righteousness. Three of my uncles and one of my sisters chose the consecrated life and lived it joyfully, showing me that God's love is real and powerful enough to sustain an abundantly happy life. Father Marion Schutten and Father Robert Ignatius Guste hopefully smile upon my efforts from heaven, knowing that their lives of loving service to God blessed me. Father Jules Guste, Society of our Mother of Peace, and Sister Melanie Anne Guste, Religious of the Sacred Heart, continue to inspire me by their energetic devotion to evangelization.

Thanks to early education with the gentle Religious of the Sacred Heart, I never knew a God of wrath or vengeance, and still love the beauty of Catholic traditions and Catholic teaching as they were meant to be lived. The Cenacle Sisters provided me sacred space for retreat throughout my adult life, offering sanctuary once a year from a busy houseful of a husband, four sons, and one daughter. The Jesuits led me in the Spiritual Exercises of St. Ignatius, which I consider a gift to mankind as great as the Sistine Chapel. The exercises are a treat for the soul. More recently, Fr. Joel Martin, O.S.B. has become a member of our family, parenting all of us with his jovial spirit. He lovingly offers eternal welcome at the Abbey in Cullman, AL. In Theological studies in Boston, several ground-breaking theologians inspired me. Avery Dulles, S.J., in a Masters Class on Faith and

Revelation concentrating on Epistemology, changed my perceptions about the experience of faith. Richard McBrien, S.J. gave an inspiring course on the Church. Phyllis Trible explored feminine images of God in the Old Testament. Courses with R.S.C.J. scholars Katherine Sullivan, Cora Brady and Adele Fiske had a deep impact. Formal in-depth analysis of the Old Testament and New Testament with Dr. Brant Pitre at Notre Dame Seminary aided me greatly in studying the texts, as opposed to interacting with them in personal prayer. I am deeply grateful for his scholarship.

Friends and angels too numerous to mention have made this volume possible. Among them are Sister Marina Aranzabal, S.T.J., Mary Jane Becker of Catholic Women in Action, Ninette Edmiston and Betsy Miller of the Children of Mary, St. Joseph's Abbey Retreat Center, Paulette Renaudin of the Central Service Team of Magnificat, and Anne Komly of the Catholic Bookstore in New Orleans. My husband of thirty years, Ralph, my grown children, Robert, Peter and Cee Cee, Maria, John and James have taught me a lot about God's fidelity in all circumstances.

Last but not least are my technical assistants. My daughter Maria generously assisted my search for the images and arranged for the rights pertaining to their use. She has been a heroic participant in the final product of **Being There.** I also thank Rachel Perez for her initial search for images – a huge help. Thank you to Kay Menick at Art Resource, Camilla Laib at The Hope Gallery, and the team at Westbow Press. Thank you dear Blessed Mother Mary for sending so many of your favorite angels to help this work come to fruition.

AUTHOR'S NOTE

When Saint Veronica stepped through a boisterous crowd to offer a linen cloth to wipe the face of Our Lord Jesus Christ as He climbed the hill to Calvary, she was responding to the prompting of the Spirit of the living God moving in her heart in the immediate moment. She observed His need, observed the outpouring of blood, sweat, and tears from His Holy Face, and bravely made her way through a jostling crowd of husky and merciless men in order to console Him even for a brief moment.

That gesture of bravery and compassion yielded for us an imprint of the suffering face of Jesus, the Veil of Veronica. Also known as the Sudarium, the latin word for sweat-cloth, this veil is considered a first class relic. Housed in the Vatican, the veil has been associated with numerous miracles over the centuries.

Veronica had no inkling of the historical significance of her gesture. She simply acted with urgency upon feeling the movement of the spirit of love within her in the moment when she found herself within reach of Jesus, the Lord.

Prompted by the spirit of love, I offer you these reflections on the scenes of the Mysteries of the Rosary. They came about before the Blessed Sacrament exposed in the Chapel of Perpetual Adoration.

During time spent in meditation, I entered into these history-making scenes with my mind's eye. With study of 1st century Jewish culture providing a backdrop, biblical accounts came to life. The Spiritual Exercises of St. Ignatius, notes from gifted retreat masters, theology study, and the readings of the day all helped the scriptural narratives come alive. Each reflection is a story told from the voice of one of the individuals chosen to be present when the great epiphanies defining Jesus as Lord took place.

This work is offered to you with the hope of enriching and enlivening your time spent in prayer. As stories are told within these pages, you may find yourself conjuring your own images and impressions of the scenes, picturing them happening as if you were there.

These meditations represent one Catholic Christian's rendering of moments in time destined to be remembered by billions of Christians the world over. While the poetry emerges from the foundation of lifetime use of the Rosary in prayer and informal and formal study of Catholic Biblical theology, it is important to note that they are not offered as teaching, strictly speaking, but as tools for personal prayer. Nothing in these pages should conflict with or contradict in any way the Catholic Christian dogma supplied by the Catechism of the Catholic Church. The slightest derogation from the teachings of the Magisterium would be outside the intention of my writing. Poetry is an art form supplying a lens for reaching into the spiritual realm.

In closing, I extend to you, my prayerful readers, these wishes:

May the Lord Jesus continue to nourish you in your hunger for His Truth, Peace, Justice, and Mercy. May Mary our Mother be present with you in joyful times, and come quickly to console you during difficult challenges of life. May communion with God's Holy Spirit satisfy your thirst for Divine grace.

Being There At The Scene Of

The Joyful Mysteries

THE FIRST JOYFUL MYSTERY

THE ANNUNCIATION

The Angel Gabriel Brings News to the Blessed Virgin Mary

"Hail, full of grace, the Lord is with you! ...Do not be afraid, Mary, for you have found favor with God." Luke 1: 28-30

One to Come

Quieted in the brilliance
Of the morning sun, I was
Invited by a fragrance
Near the earth

To bow low, kiss sweet petals,
And praise my God Who made them.
In that moment
It was delivered

Unto me – a girl so small!
The Word.

Seized by the truth
So near my womb, I gasped
"It cannot be!"
Yet He gave Word.

In the warmth,
In the quiet,
In the light, I heard it clearly.
Word that the Word

Wanted to be within me.
The One to come
Was very near and
Needing only me.

Needing me!
So small
To house His light
Infinite world-changing radiance.

"My God, You ask me
To bring forth
Your Son, the Son of Man
The universal Light?"

I stretch forward and wonder how,
Embrace the earth like my mother,
Finger the fragile petals drifted to earth – so like myself.

The lovely wings of a little white dove
Stop their flapping.
He alights nearby
He seems to wait.
I smile into the eyes

Of my winged friend.
"Oh Yes! Yes! Yes!" I exclaim it.
Rolling back to take warm rays
I know the One to come

Is here.

The Annunciation by the Angel to Joseph in a Dream

"…behold, an angel of the Lord appeared to him in a dream, saying, 'Joseph, son of David, do not fear to take Mary your wife, for that which is conceived in her is of the Holy Spirit.'" Matthew 1: 20

JOSEPH SPEAKS

The Annunciation to Saint Joseph

At the very least to temple I had been.
Seen scrolls sewn together, read aloud
All expounding, but only confounding
The simple boy I was.

She was but a girl when I first gazed upon her.
A split second and I knew the God of Whom they spoke.
The God Who was for me, Who made me man that day –
That instant!

I saw Him in her hands,
Her cheek, her chin, her shoulders.
I felt that same God greet me
When she turned to look at my face.

I took my stand then
To forever remain
Precariously perched between
Humility and humiliation,
In manly and meek serenity.
Honored, not crushed.

I chop wood while
She meets God.

But oh! I had my angels!
They bore strange news. Good tidings,
Evil forebodings, directions, plans, roadmaps.
Knowledge of the One above and His onerous, awful mission
For me – to protect, to serve and oh! To rule the ruler,
The child God!

At least they spoke, my friends the angels!
Without them it would have been a quick dive
Into eternal humiliation!
They sang to me to calm my heart.
They spoke to me to light the way.
They frolicked in my mind as on a lawn,
Helped me to laugh in the face of the un–manly fear
Who crept up around my heart like a snake
To whisper in sardonic glee
That I was nothing but a lunatic,
And she a wasted woman
Descended from nobility.

I chop wood
While she meets God!

This was not my plan!
What to do? Where to go?
I am but a man!
My angels didn't wait to come.
Fleeting they came – faith-filled and filling me.

I knew they would call us The Holy Family.
The angels told me why.
But one solitary human in the clan threatened
Some slight gulf between the title
And the reality. That one being me.

I was told to make her leave
Many times.
I was instructed in clear terms,
Told I must insist, when
I knew the pain it would cause her
The love who bore my God!

At times I had to see she stayed
When she begged to leave.
The lovely ways of angels
Were not bestowed upon me.
This she didn't really understand.
My angels only spoke to me!
They made things clear.

God. You made my life a constant plea for help!
And now I rest, my chopping done.
And I meet God – face to face!
And dance with angels!
With Him, with her, with all the saints –
Ecstasy!
Never sinking to my
Human reality,
But seizing its essence
From a distance
In transcendence.

THE SECOND JOYFUL MYSTERY

THE VISITATION

Mary Visits with her Cousin Elizabeth

"And when Elizabeth heard the greeting of Mary, the child leaped in her womb…and she exclaimed with a loud cry, 'Blessed are you among women and blessed is the fruit of your womb!'" Luke 1: 41-42

And You Too!

The Visitation with Elizabeth

From afar
I spotted her
Coming my way, large
With the child
In her womb.

Reaching my hand
To the sky
To signal her,
My little one leapt
For the first time.

This awaited flip
Affirmed the Word
Of One to come;
The movement spoke
Wonders filling my heart
For the ages.

The hand of the Almighty
Is upon her.
The babe within me will announce Him,
And He will renew the face of the earth.

My cousin sounds a singing, ringing,
Knowing call of recognition,
Of Alleluia
As she approaches.

I am coming, coming and quickening.
I call to her
With heart and lips crying
"And you, too!"

THE THIRD JOYFUL MYSTERY

THE BIRTH OF OUR LORD

The Savior is Brought Forth in Bethlehem

"And she gave birth to her firstborn son and wrapped him in swaddling cloths, and laid him in a manger, because there was no place for them in the inn." Luke 2: 7

The Trip

Mary and Joseph Travel to Bethlehem for the Birth of the Savior

The animal they loaned to us was docile and complacent.
I wondered even so – how would this ever work? I climbed
On. We left our home, thinking it was to Bethlehem we would go,
Not knowing it was to heaven! The beast beneath me plodded ever
So deliberately, as with a sense of stealth and with care, rhythm, and
Delicate concern, as if he knew. His care was God's care
And my heart poured forth my thanks while
A rocking motion propelled us forward.
Our little group of three - no, four - moved together.
Joseph's hand was ever locked with mine.

As we journeyed in the cold, crisp night our hearts were one
In peace and joy, as though drawn by love with our souls aspiring
to the rest of it.
Somewhere it was along the way, no one could ever say where,
It happened that our souls were unleashed and blended into a unity,
Becoming a family.
Then, we possessed heaven in the mere anticipation
Of the babe's appearance, which we knew was to come.

Together we moved forward in silence with great care, in
This time, place, and body. But our souls were everywhere around
The universe. One minute with the cherubim and seraphim
Singing out – our hearts and voices telling of the glory land to be.
Unlikely dreams befuddled me, dreams of being crowned a queen!

It was the trip of our lifetime. A trip to transform human life
For all time. For all men and women. It seemed as though
They were there with us somehow.
We went with a different idea.

Constant was his hand in mine,
Constant the faint sound of plodding in
Soft earth, helping our spirits come loose from bodily creation.
This departure had been saved. A surprise to lift the spirit from the
Frame. We left simply to register, knowing too that it may be
To bring forth the babe far from home.
Sensations began to tell me of His descent into our midst.
Our spirits ascended, Joseph's surged with mine and we went
Soaring, dying 'round His throne until we were right there –
Nestled within a blessed trinity pushing forth an incarnation and
Having only frozen tears to remind us that this was real
In human terms. We came to the hay.

It looked to me like the bed chambers I had heard about
In gilded cities far away, but more perfect – so blessed with peace
Serenity, the cleanliness of earth, and sky and air, the sight of stars
The midnight blue firmament, the purity of the animals in there.
This refuge became my little temple, the meeting place of
Man and God.

Then it was happening – my king had begun His descent into
Our midst. My spirit joined with a throng all around the universe
Singing praise, joining light, rising to glory
Enthralled to recognize Incarnation.
Then the universe was in my arms.
I wrapped my warmth around him
And knew what had been there before time.

The cry of the babe pierced open the firmament.
God's power crashed into our hearts.
Infinity was placed in my arms.
It was an end for mankind, and a beginning.

Our spirits danced in unison. God has given us a son!
"For unto us a child is born,"
As the prophet had foretold.
God had broken the veil of the known,
Broken through our material world to push His personhood into it.

It was really the trip of our lives.
We never did come back.

Gabriel, I think, had not forgotten to tell all this.
He held it as a surprise to be given in God's time.

We left for a city, we arrived in Paradise.
And took Him with us everywhere. Always.
For the rest of time.
And into eternity.

THE THIRD JOYFUL MYSTERY

THE BIRTH OF THE SAVIOR

*The Music Filling the Earth and the Heavens
as the Savior is Brought Forth*

"And suddenly there was with the angel a multitude of the heavenly host praising God and saying, 'Glory to God in the highest, and on earth peace among men with whom He is pleased!" Luke 2: 13-14

Music from the Manger

I, the field dog, friend to the shepherd,
stood still as never before,
my canine ears receiving sounds
of a heavenly host while

I, the bovine beast, brushed royal robes,
nudged at the feet of a tiny babe, breathed
the king's incense and entered heaven's chorus
with lowing sounds.

I, the shepherd, shielded my eye
to look up, behold
power and light pour forth
from a familiar star. I dropped to my knees.
Time was no more.

I, a king, came in search
of another one.
It led me to enter the story, the
music for ages to come.

I, the star, shed light announcing Him
embracing You. Together we sing
heaven's sweet whisperings, filling silence
with splendor – silent night, holy night.

I, the angel, look on from above
a filter of heaven's ineffable love.

I, Joseph, looked at my wife and the Babe
curled in my arms, and
knew it was done, knew only hope with
the victory of man tucked in my embrace.

I, Mother Mary, looked at the Babe,
beheld only a sea of shining light,
a blinding vision. I looked at the snow but
felt only fire.

Together we sing ecstatic music of the manger,
sweet unction to heal and make holy,
to pierce the most hardened heart,
the mixed melody heard only in death –
silent night, holy night.

THE FOURTH JOYFUL MYSTERY

THE PRESENTATION OF THE INFANT JESUS IN THE TEMPLE

The Infant Savior is Anointed by the Prophet Simeon

"…he took him up into his arms and blessed God and said, 'Lord, now let your servant depart in peace, according to your word; for my eyes have seen your salvation…a light for revelation to the Gentiles, and for glory to your people Israel.'" Luke 2: 28-30, 32

Simeon Remembers

The Presentation of the Infant Jesus in the Temple

Stepping through the city gates,
Assuming the persona, a prince of the priestly caste,
Perched in peace-filled pride,
The Word of God like fire had burnt through to
Each infant rolled into my arms by
Frightened, new parents, hopeful,
Banking on One-to-Come soon.
Daily the blessed water flowed, names were given, hearts
burnished
Records collected, history and memory built.
Ours was a cult of waiting.

Day after day, month after month, year after year
The stream of humanity continued.
Fire burned in my soul, gleamed, marked hearts.
The children came, went, grew, flourished
And died, some of them, before my eyes
Until I wondered, "How long will You have me here,
O Mighty One,
For my hands are weary, and my limbs are weakened."
"Stay and wait. Nothing has changed. All is illusion.
Time withering flesh
Creates illusion.
It is always new." Came the answer.

Mine the duty to be there. I remember
Sameness of gestures, blessings, touch, sharing joy.
I was like a column of the temple, conferring identity.
A word like a flame flickered inside, "Wait for me. You will
know me."

For the sake of the prophets, for the sake of the people of Israel
For the Mighty One who Spoke, I needed to stay.
With wisdom written on the walls of my soul,
Illusion made me a decrepit, laughable, leathery old fool with
A crazed glow in his eyes.

The last stretch before the dawn, no matter the weakness
The conviction of His nearness grew, solid and sturdy as the limbs
rusted.

Then came the day of His glory, firmament singing,
Sun burning warm
Brisk breeze brushing bringing goose-flesh,
The day of His dawning blazed brilliant hours before the family
arrived.
A joy-filled confusion, heaven revealed itself all around and inside
Truth surged up from within, stabled with force – this knowing!

Stretching my arms, reaching forth to heaven in praise
I was beside myself.
"This is the day the Lord has made!
Let us rejoice and be glad in it!"
Be glad! Be glad! And I was filled with gladness overflowing until
There showed on the horizon the precious, huddling
Moving bundle of salvation.
Three blessed ones – father, mother and babe
Coming toward me as one.
The sight, imprinted upon the walls of my soul,
Emblazoned a new image of truth, as had the words of long ago:
"Wait for me."

Meaning radiated around the threesome, light grew more intense,
Surrounding skies ringing alleluia,
The everydayness of the scene scintillated anew
With expectation fulfilled; simple folk going about
Business came to life triple-fold, radiance illuminating
The usual steps in the path.

Then glory was in my leathery arms.
He was a babe wrapped in the usual way.
"How, O Mighty One, why, O Mighty One?
You, here, in my human embrace,
On an ordinary day in this neglected village?"
Her eyes so sweet, arms so short and small, pouring His baby body
Into my old man's hands,
Presenting, offering, giving and receiving blessing, confirming all.
Before I could blink evening was upon me,
The evening of peace-filling
When I was given leave, departed, and awoke at home.

THE FIFTH JOYFUL MYSTERY

THE FINDING OF THE CHILD JESUS IN THE TEMPLE

The Boy Jesus is Found Teaching in the Jerusalem Temple

"After three days they found him in the temple, sitting among the teachers, listening to them and asking them questions; and all who heard him were amazed at his understanding and his answers." Luke 2: 46–47

Lost and Found

Before we could ask
"Who let go", we were
Racing like two rickety maniacs
Returning to Jerusalem.

Snapped from our connection, the
Incompleteness dismembering
Our sensation of unity, madness in the flight
Challenged the limit of limbs.

The demons fled alongside at our feet.
The Fury at one another yelling out "Who's to blame?"
The Anger at His abandonment clawed.
The Worry demon nearly knocked me to the ground: "Is He alive?"

"Did He trip on the road? Was there water, food?
Was he devoured by a leopard? Wild cat?
Poisoned by bandits? Stampeded?
In the city, was there a mat?"

The demons wanted Him,
The demons wanted Joseph and me
To die, to be crushed, to be apart,
To lose faith in one another.

While the serpent clawed at my feet with
Doubts, fears, agitation, anger (Run! Quick!),
The image of my Son, the emerging man,
Drew me forward.

The demon Disappointment rapped my brain:
"He knew what He was doing. He always does!"

The demon Hurt: "Why did He abandon us?"
Then came God's answer –
"He is beyond the two of you!"
The demon Brokenness entered, from our being apart.

Crossing the threshold of the Temple
I laid eyes on our child
Nearing His time to become a man,
The serpent fell. The three of us were one again.

And it was grace.
He didn't say "Pardon me, Father, Mother."
What He did not say counted to tell me
We were supposed to know.

SUGGESTIONS FOR REFLECTION, DISCUSSION, AND
JOURNALING

The First Joyful Mystery - The Annunciation

"One to Come" and "Joseph Speaks"

1) In what settings am I most capable of attuning myself
   to God's Word for me? Where do I feel His Presence
   most powerfully?

2) Do I cultivate and remain faithful to habits which
   help me to experience God's loving Presence on a
   regular basis?

3) Are there prayer tools, aids, and materials which may
   be of help in focusing my attunement to God's word
   for me and His work in me?

4) Am I scheduling my prayer and creating an agenda
   so meticulously that I cannot simply listen to the
   movement of the Spirit?

5) Have I created a niche within my home where I can
   center myself in relationship with the Lord?

6) Use the narrative in "Joseph Speaks" to contemplate,
   and imagine what it would be like to live right
   alongside Jesus on a day-to-day basis, realizing the
   Christ Child's sinless, Divine Nature?

The Second Joyful Mystery - The Visitation

"And You Too"

1) Who is the individual to whom you turn immediately when there is important life-changing news, such as a birth, a death or a crisis?

2) Who are several others, the chosen few, with whom you would soon share such special news, joyful or sorrowful?

3) How do I celebrate that relationship and keep it alive with mutual sharing and support?

4) In the crowded schedule of life, do I become neglectful of sacred relationships which ignite recognition of God's awesome presence in our lives?

5) Are there temptations or distractions that lead me to dissipate my attention from my loved ones?

The Third Joyful Mystery - The Birth of the Lord

"The Trip"

1) Try to envision St. Ann's attitude, posture, demeanor, the look on her face or in her eyes? Imagine St. Joachim's behavior.

2) In taking leave of home, Mary and Joseph clearly parted with physical comfort. When has God asked me to part with physical comfort? How do I adapt to that?

3) When last did I deliberately leave my comfort zone for love or duty?

4) When God's requests, directions, or commands seem difficult or even impossible, how do I find childlike surrender and trust?

5) As you read "The Trip," which images and details were different from your usual imaginings?

6) Are there areas in my life where I need to surrender and let go, even without an extraordinary situation to make it necessary? Is there a relationship where I need to be less "in control"?

"The Music of the Manger"

1) What did you see, hear, or feel there that you have never noticed or sensed before? Sounds? Textures? Odors? The darkness? The air quality? Did you notice where the light came from?

2) Was anyone else there besides the attendants at the traditional crèche scene which we are accustomed to? Perhaps a woman from the nearby inn who was aware of the onset of Mary's labor?

3) Describe the sound of the music you heard.

4) What were your emotions there? Anything new?

5) Describe your experience at the manger in a letter to a friend. Go back to the scene and "be there" for a little while before you compose your letter.

The Fourth Joyful Mystery - The Presentation of the Child Jesus in the Temple

"Simeon Remembers"

1) When I awake in the morning, do I consciously expect God to manifest Himself to me in the course of the day?

2) Are there specific tools or reminders which I could use in order to make sure I turn my attention to God immediately upon waking?

3) Could I create a habit of praising Him for that anticipated gift right away, even before it arrives?

4) What does the elder Simeon have to say to you? Does your job or vocation begin to seem mechanical, as though it doesn't have the same feeling it did when you began?

The Fifth Joyful Mystery - The Finding of the Child Jesus in the Temple

"Lost and Found"

1) If my children are presently very small, how can I prepare for the day when they must enter into their own vocations in life?

2) Do I feel panic or anger when my child roams away from me?

3) There will be times in every parent's life when a child is missing. Am I prepared to trust God's guardianship? How do I train myself to call upon the Lord immediately?

4) When a child is missing, or even just wandering from the beaten path, do I remember that the Blessed Mother had the very same challenges?

5) All children eventually must break away from their parents, and follow God's call and God's path for them. Am I exceedingly possessive of my children, or do I accept the fact that they have their orders from God which will carry them away from me?

Being There At The Scene Of

The Luminous Mysteries

The First Luminous Mystery

The Baptism of Jesus in the River Jordan

John the Baptist Blesses the King of Kings in the Jordan

"John would have prevented him saying,
'I need to be baptized by you and do you come to me?'
But Jesus answered him, 'Let it be so now; for thus it is fitting for us
to fulfil all righteousness.'" Matthew 3: 14-15

Bringing in the King

The Baptism of Jesus as told by John the Baptist

From near and far they filed in reliably each day
Responding to my call: "Prepare ye the way of the Lord!"
The sages spoke of it, the priests – unsettled, excited
Buzzed on, as news of the One-to-Come filtered down.

God's people came in waves morning to night
To repent, be born again, cleansed, made new.
Repentant hearts filled up with waters from
The river of heaven's mercy.

For this stretch of the way, my work was to pour and to pronounce.
Pour waters of God's life and love on these
Courageous penitents. Pronounce them clean, strong,
Free, ready, belonging among the Chosen.

From years of penitence and privation in the caves nearby
Came my strength and the nerve to water them.
I was the priest without appointment, the harbinger of
The new Way of Salvation.

Those at Temple
Were not pleased with me.
Not one bit.
But still God's people came.

At dawn on that morning, the morn of my Lord's appearance,
An azure sky drew my heart heavenward.
Droves of doves filled the firmament
Flapping and dancing as though celebrating an occasion.

Angels hiding just behind the veil of the visible
Hummed a thrilling "Gloria!"
Over and over, in languages foreign to my ears.
Did others hear it too?

Beholding his entourage, my heart stood at attention.
Instructions concerning this moment of revelation
Had been given to me long ago in the caves at Qumran.
My resistance had proven fruitless.

This dreaded duty bore down on me like a curse.
In this assignment, I must own all of my sinfulness,
The sin nature I had so suffered to put down and conquer.
In this chore I must face my failure, my unwillingness,

My humanity, my brokenness, the sin of Adam within me still.
On the other days, I had felt myself the one victorious over all of it,
The very catalyst of conversion.
My hands seemed the hands of God, washing and welcoming.

From afar, the company of Jesus moved toward me.
Knees weakened.
I stood in my appointed spot,
And surrendered to the inevitable.

His atmosphere of light approached,
A mist of grace surrounded Him.
Who was the baptizer and who the baptized?
Oh, this confusion!

Lifting my cupped hands over His Divine Head,
My arms seemed impossibly heavy, weighted with all of my humanity.
But my shame, like thickened rust in these joints,
Did not prevail.

I did what I had to do.

As the new King of Kings was born anew
In waters of His own Divinity
Graciousness in the form of a lone and radiant dove
Settled above my royal cousin Jesus like a crown.

And others heard the sound that reached my ears:
"This is My beloved Son in whom I am well pleased!"

The words bathed my soul, as well as His own,
In un-hoped for new Life.

Cooperating, yielding to the Divine request
I had managed to bring in the King!

The Second Luminous Mystery

The Wedding Feast at Cana

"His Mother said to the servants, 'Do whatever he tells you.'" John 2: 5

The Advocate's Blessing

The Wedding Feast at Cana: The Blessed Mother Prompts Jesus' First Miracle

Father did not come that day.
Such celebrations were difficult for him.
He would stay and work on an order.

Mother and I attended for the family,
And everyone understood.
Spirits were high. It seemed a perfect match –
The daughter of Mother's cousin to wed
A prospering young merchant.

Occasions such as these bode well for all –
Our clan would continue to grow and thrive
And the young would carry on traditions.
Spirits were high with the goodness of life, and
Being a people blessed.
Favored by God in being just where we were.
Yahweh's Chosen. Set aside for special things to come.

Mother took delight in others.
Many treasured a moment near her.
Quiet jubilation flowed from her small frame.
Enigmas surrounded her, a peaceful but compelling mystery
Attracted others to approach her delicately,
Behave in her presence, nod deference,
Yearn for her approval.
Stories had circulated. She held a long foretold promise,
The secret of our royalty.

To move among others was to know more
Of the God she loved so dearly.
To touch others was to share refreshment of life,
The Holy Spirit of Life which surrounded my Mother, Mary.
Natural and grace–filled was her enjoyment.

Father marveled at her ease with God's children.
The folks she mingled with had nothing in common with her.
He wondered – should not her mystery be set apart?

During the lengthy repast friends and family reclined
To take part in a feast of life,
Folklore came alive again,
The joy in sharing memories and hopes
Multiplied during the hours of regaling.
As uncles and cousins began to arise, sway, toddle, and tilt
To lean on one another, our neighbors at table whispered
That the wine was out.

Mother turned to me, leaned close and spoke with her eyes.
Seldom was Mother so serious with me.
Long ago, I had come to independence.
Even as the guests swaggered about jovial and gay,
She behaved as though the shortage were a matter of urgency.
"They have no more wine!" she whispered,
Desperate to save her cousin and the bride from shame.

"Mother, my hour has not yet come." I replied.
As though she did not hear me, she instructed the servants:
"Do whatever He tells you."

Quiet authority established destiny. I submitted.
The servants turned to me expectantly.
"Fill those jugs with water."
With palm of hand facing heaven to catch drops of grace,
I pointed to the empty jugs.

In the revelry of the new wine it seemed that no one noticed.
However, the steward remembered it well.

THE THIRD LUMINOUS MYSTERY

THE PROCLAMATION OF THE KINGDOM OF GOD

Jesus Declares the Fulfillment of Prophecy is at Hand

"Today this Scripture has been fulfilled in your hearing." Luke 4: 21

Rock of Grace

The Proclamation of the Kingdom of God As Witnessed by a Cousin of Jesus.

He stood to receive the Holy Book and read.
I shuddered.
My cousin, my childhood playmate.
Shuddered not only to observe His stature
So like a king,
His bodily frame uncommonly straight, tall
His broad shoulders,
His face, beautiful since childhood, become that of a man.
A man of royal lineage.
Shuddered not only to remember the enigma
Of His childlike ways of days past
When things happened in His presence.
Things you could not explain in any way.
Not even the wisest among us had a clue –
A suffering aunt cured,
A storm driven away on festival day –
Except that in every case our cousin Jesus had
Looked to heaven in that wordless way, conversing
In silence with His Father,
Not even a nod of the head,
Simply trusting, waiting.

I shuddered to observe my cousin arise in the synagogue
And open the Scriptures,
Knowing well what our brethren the Pharisees
Did with false prophets, magicians, heretics, the unclean.
It would be the worst, no doubt, not only because of His power
But because of what people were saying of Him.
And because He would only answer questions with the truth.

43

Something strong inside me tumbled
And shattered into a million pieces.
To know what they would do
To the beautiful human being there before me.

The stonings, the beatings, the hangings.
It began to seem like giving the common folk something to do.

But here He was before me, the Holy Book in His upturned hands
So like a mighty rock of grace.
Many a gift flowed from His eyes,
Gifts which stopped you in your tracks,
Changed your heart, your view of the world.
He made me remember the God of Abraham, our God of promise,
Our amazing sense of being God's chosen.
Beholding Him, you remembered our God,
And you met Him in a new form —
In human form.
Eerie to many.
To those who knew our traditions the most, it was frightening.
One needed to decide what to do about it — Him.
To count oneself in His ranks would clearly be a risk.

Jesus spoke: "He sent me to proclaim release to the captives
And recovering of sight to the blind,
To set at liberty those who are oppressed,
And to proclaim the acceptable year of the Lord."

I saw the unraveling history of man
Sprawled out across the firmament,
Lanced by a dagger of supernatural light —
A shocking light, illuminating the panorama evolving across time.

Then He sealed His fate,
"Today this Scripture has been fulfilled in your hearing."

My cousin, my childhood playmate!
His grandfather Jacob the brother of mine.
And I, Joseph, bore the name of His father Joseph.
It was a small town for such portentous happenings.
Had we all gone mad with the waiting?

I heard a mighty sound shaking heaven and earth – a chorus
Ringing round the world and shouting powerfully:
"For unto us a child is born, a Son is given!
And His name shall be called
Wonderful! Counselor!
Almighty God, the everlasting Father,
The Prince of peace."
I heard it and I know I heard it.
A mighty ringing throng shouting out
This proclamation
In glorious music.

I blinked and all were gone from the synagogue.
There was screaming in the street.
I moved to the entryway, watched as
The angry mob chased my rock of grace away.
I shuddered to think what was next.

The Fourth Luminous Mystery

The Transfiguration of Jesus

The Transfiguration Remembered by the Apostle James

"...Jesus took with him Peter and James and John, and led them up a high mountain apart by themselves; and he was transfigured before them, and his garments became glistening, intensely white...." Mark 9: 2-3

Becoming the Bread Which Rises Before Us

The Transfiguration of our Lord as Witnessed by the Apostle James

He said it once again–
"Follow me."
Addressing John and Peter
And me.

It was almost too much.
Did our Brother
Consider our human moments?
He swirled to enter the climb.

He held a mystery
To be sure.
That confidence in
Knowing we would do His bidding.

Leather soles of sandals
Mother-crafted
Were past worn, as we ourselves were.
The craggy mountainside ripped them mercilessly.

Is this necessary?
Peter and John and I
Thought in unison.
Shoulders kept at work, pulling

Torsos angled forward and upward,
We became a trudging train
Of His inner circle
Moving to an intimate place

To view the secret wonder.
Little did we know,
Little did we know what would come- a vision of heaven
Atop the mountain beside Him.

Our lordly cousin
Knew so much,
Could do so much!
We would follow Him anywhere.
"This could be dangerous!"
Peter exclaimed.
"This IS dangerous!"
John spoke quietly.

Still we continued upward,
Knees cracking,
Feet digging
Into the rocks.

At last He stood still –
Close to the peak.
Clouds drifted about, encircling,
Draping His human form.

His white robes lifted
Joining the sheer grace of the whiteness
Surrounding us.
Like bread which rises

His human form became transfigured
Joining nature's movements
And supernature's privilege.
The vision we possessed in common changed history.

The three of us –
Simple-minded humans
Witnessed Him join heaven thus,
Felt heaven collide and merge with humanness

Before us there
Was no confusion or mistake,
No doubt or fear left possible.
The three of us were one in this.

THE FIFTH LUMINOUS MYSTERY

THE INSTITUTION OF THE EUCHARIST

Jesus' Last Supper with His Apostles in the Upper Room As Told by the Apostle Peter

"And as they were eating, he took bread, and blessed, and broke it, and gave it to them, and said, 'Take; this is my body.'" Mark 14: 22

Last Night, First Night

The Institution of the Eucharist told by the Apostle Peter

Night fell too soon. Who could be ready?
Complete were arrangements
According to the Master's instructions.
We had been warned in no uncertain terms
Devastation was upon us.

Our Master, Lord of Life, Lord of Creation, Lord of Lords –
The One Who had become our New Life, our Way
Would be handed over near midnight.
This evening's meal – a supper of love, communion, and farewell.

Taking the stairs to the Upper Room two by two
A turbulent storm spun about in my heart.
Gruesome fear strapped down upon my back.
Excitement bubbled, heated up as in a cauldron, mixed with terror

Causing a blinding smoke as I moved up to the Cenacle.
Sorrow swirled in with deepest tender love.
Horror welled up as images of torture
Made their way past the wall I built to keep them out.

Jesus had plucked me for His Rock.
He gave to me keys to the kingdom
The power to loose and to bind.
When He would leave us
I was to take His place, build His Church.
On this night of our Last Supper, I was anything but a rock.

How greatly I longed to go with Him, my strength!
Only near Him could I pull through
To fulfill the awesome commission.
In His presence I became what I was not.
With Him, I became what He made me to be.

Moments collide in retrospect. Soon as His own gathered,
He was going from one to the next with towel and basin,
Washing our stinking feet.
The God–Man, Purity and Light in Person,
On knees before me? No!
Dread! His Godliness must never touch my filthy feet,
My grimy manhood!
"You shall never touch my feet!" I protested.
Insisting, He broke past pride, fear and all my defenses.
I surrendered in disbelief – covered in soot and sin.
The sublime compassion of His hands upon my feet
Taught me the meaning of love,
Taught all of us our new way of service.

The exposure seemed hard to bear.
He knew me as no better than the rest.
Weak. I am too weak! When he departs, I cannot be strong!
Can it be that He does not know this?
But He read my mind and pinned me clearly:

"Truly, truly, the cock will not crow
Till you have denied me three times!"
The heart within me sank and drowned.
Before too long He offered: "Do not let your hearts be troubled.
Peace I leave with you. My peace I give to you."

He broke the bread and blessed it, saying "This is my Body,
Which is given for you."
We shared it quietly.
"This is my blood of the Covenant,
Which is poured out for many."
The cup was passed.

Events flow together in memory.
Friends dispersed in the darkness.
The night of communion and love was finished.
The night of passion had begun.

Suggestions for Reflection, Discussion, and Journaling

The First Luminous Mystery - The Baptism of Jesus by John the Baptist

"Bringing in the King"

1) What do you recall about the relationship of John the Baptist and Jesus from their childhood? Growing up as cousins whose mothers were the closest of friends, how do you think this affected the two cousins? Have you imagined them at family reunions, weddings etc. when extended family was present?

2) What other experiences as young men developing their spiritual life did John share with Jesus?

3) Why do you suppose it was an onerous and burdensome assignment for John the Baptist to officially baptize Jesus in the Jordan before other penitents?

4) What are some responsibilities which God calls you to carry out that are particularly difficult for you? These could be worldly duties of our station in life, or duties of service required of us, as in the spiritual or corporal works of mercy.

5) What channels of grace help the most to keep faithful to discharging these God-given tasks? e.g. classes, spiritual direction, visiting special blessed places and sanctuaries.

6) Like Jesus and John the Baptist, there are those who become our "spiritual friends." How do I affirm them and send them into God's work? Do I pray for them regularly? Do I take steps to strengthen them in their mission?

The Second Luminous Mystery - The Wedding Feast at Cana

"The Advocate's Blessing"

1) Recall your different emotions and reactions as you heard Jesus tell about His Mother.

2) Is it natural, normal or unorthodox to equate the state of grace with elation in the "joie-de-vivre?"

3) Why do you think Mary made an unusual request of her Son to begin His career with a miracle for such a seemingly worldly reason?

4) Why did Jesus defer to her?

5) What does this scene reveal about Mary's influence with Jesus for our personal prayers, hopes, dreams and needs?

6) Is anything too foolish to ask for? Do you feel that Mary loves you as her own child, and would ask Jesus for anything that was good for you?

The Third Luminous Mystery - The Proclamation of the Kingdom of God

"Rock of Grace"

1) Those present at this scene were stunned, awestruck and frightened by Jesus' audacious proclamation of the fulfillment of prophecy.
Do I feel struck with the awesome power which is manifested at the altar at Mass each time the Eucharist is transformed through transubstantiation?

2) Have you ever felt fright along with awe? When?

3) After Jesus announced the Scriptures fulfilled in their hearing, he needed to escape quickly in order to avoid being stoned to death.
Do I face consequences in certain places if I proclaim the Good News of Jesus as the Messiah? Does mere unpopularity bother me?

4) When do I pronounce the Word of God loudly and unhesitatingly?

5) When must I leave a safety zone to proclaim Christ as the Savior?

The Fourth Luminous - Mystery The Transfiguration

"Becoming the Bread Which Rises Before Us"

1) What are a few natural settings which give you a sense of the spiritual realm? Where have you most deeply felt surrounded by Gods indwelling presence, mystery and majesty?

2) Are there certain times of the day when you feel it is easiest to experience the holiness of God's creation?

3) Do you maintain a habit of tracking down these peak moments of communion with God in His natural world?

4) Peter, John and James were the apostles who were closest to the Lord.
Do you feel that there was something in particular that each one of them did to receive this honor?

5) What means do I take regularly to seek intimacy with Jesus?

6) What responsibility did this close friendship give to them, and to me?

The Fifth Luminous Mystery – The Institution of the Eucharist

"Last Night, First Night"

1) Peter raced up the stairs to the Cenacle with excitement in anticipation of the events of the evening in front of him.
What is my level of anticipatory joy or thrill when I am going to participate in Holy Mass, and receive Holy Communion?

2) What perspective transformation can I engage in to bring about the attitude of excitement which should ideally characterize receiving this precious and holy sacrament?

3) What habits could I adopt which may reflect the reverence I wish to show with regard to the Eucharistic feast? e.g. type of dress, taking a role in altar service, become a lector, get to Mass early in order to reflect and ready oneself spiritually?

4) Is the Holy Sacrifice of the Mass central in my life? Do I teach this to others by my example?

5) Is daily Mass possible for me?

Being There At The Scene Of

The Sorrowful Mysteries

THE FIRST SORROWFUL MYSTERY

THE AGONY IN THE GARDEN

Jesus Prays Before His Trial

"Then He said to them, 'My soul is very sorrowful, even unto death; remain here, and watch with me. And going a little farther he fell on his face and prayed, 'My Father, if it be possible, let this chalice pass from me; nevertheless, not as I will, but as thou wilt." Matthew 26: 38-39

Lead, Blood, Mud

The Agony in the Garden

The sky like coal
Deep, dark, wide, infinite
Rained down heavy upon my head, neck, shoulders, back.
Both my legs had given way at sunset,
And my knees dug deep into the muddy earth
In the grove.

Tonight, my dampened head
Is free
Free from the penetrating thorns
To smash through my skull tomorrow
To circle my brain
With the sins of man,
To cruelly seduce me to renounce You

Father God!
The stars tonight send
No hope.
They too, turn on me
Sending injections of fear like needles,

And the perforations around my head
Pour fright, in drops of ink-like blood
Into the miry earth between my fingers.
Why do I grasp this fluid clay
In my desperation?

Father, is this necessary?
My shoulders long to give way

And join the earth before it all starts,
Sink into the sludge, and end it now.

Father, is this right?
Surely meant for your lamb?
For me, so much Yours,
The soul of You, in human flesh?

Father,
Are You with me?

Do You hear?
Is this it?
Can we stop this?
Now?
Now! Now, the hour
Of a coal black sky
Cruel stars telling the truth
Of tomorrow.

Branches stir in the wind
Like witches their brew.

The Father speaks at last.
"It is progress, my Son.
It has begun.
You are with me, and
I am with You.
You grasp this earth now.
Tomorrow

You will no longer
Be a part of it."

THE SECOND SORROWFUL MYSTERY

THE SCOURGING AT THE PILLAR

Jesus is Whipped by the Roman Soldiers

"So Pilate, wishing to satisfy the crowd, released for them Barabbas, and having scourged Jesus, he delivered him to be crucified." Mark 15:15

Cup of Lashes

The Scourging at the Pillar

"The cup you measure with,"
Father God, You Yourself proclaimed,
"Will be measured back to you."
In these lashes?
Father!
Where are You? The measure
Of my goodness,
Measured back, but quadrupled
Plus some, in these spiked lashes
Tearing my flesh apart?
Answer me, O God, my Dad, my Abba Father!
"It is not I who wields this whip,
My favored son, precious Lamb.
My very heart pours forth in your blood.
With Your world-changing blood,
I am washing the face of the world."
Nothing You say makes sense, Father!
Cries the Son, torn to shreds on the ground.
"Not in human terms, in human thought, no.
This blood of yours, my Son, is tears flowing
From my Heart, do you not remember?"
Father, this is not the love we share.
This is not what I came here for.
"No, it is men. Men who hate what we are."
The Father whispers.
What? What do they hate? I gave only love!
Cries the Son.
"They hate Your Power of Love.
They hate Your Beauty.
They hate what they know –
That You are changing their world."

My flesh is ravaged now.
My bones will move to You without it.

THE THIRD SORROWFUL MYSTERY

THE CROWNING WITH THORNS

The Roman Soldiers Mock Jesus with a Crown of Thorns

"And they stripped him and put a scarlet robe upon him, and plaiting a crown of thorns they put it on his head, and put a reed in his right hand." Matthew 27: 28-29

Breaking Through Open Pores

The Crowning With Thorns

Strange flaming stars
Sent to sear
Needles of Your love and pain straight
Through to my brain
Tearing through my skull.

Like a galaxy-full of tiny lances,
Thorns thrust deeply into my head
Directed by strong hands, thumbs, knuckles
Of my captors, driving them to the mark
With precision.

As the thorns, like sharp hot mini-swords,
Exploded inside my skull
Your Divine Love filled
My brain and heart, veins and arteries,
Overflowing, seeping out on the earth

Through open pores.

THE FOURTH SORROWFUL MYSTERY

THE CARRYING OF THE CROSS

Jesus Shoulders His Wooden Cross to Golgotha

"So they took Jesus, and he went out, bearing his own cross, to the place called the place of a skull, which is called in Hebrew Golgotha." John 19: 17

Nightmare Impossible

The Carrying of the Cross

Put one foot in front of the other.
Father, how?
Is not this a nightmare impossible?
With feet bloodied and bare to the bone
To put one foot forward – is - hell.
It happens anyway. It moves. I move.
Two trees roped together are saddled onto my back.
We move as in a current, slowly.
There is yelling and wailing, groaning and
Screaming all about in the crowd.
The sky is darkening.
This climb does not seem humanly possible.
These trees on my back
Should be standing in the ground giving shelter.
Instead, they give me a place to dangle and die.
My hands will be nailed to one of these trees.
My feet will be pierced and secured to the other.
Soon.
Soon as I make it to the top of the hill.
Put one foot in front of the other?

Was it supposed to end like this?
You loved me dearly as a pretty dream
And now this agony, unrelenting agony in every pore, every inch
Of my ripped up flesh,
This, my Father, is what You ask of me?
Unexpected for someone special like me.
From day one I was worshipped, thought of as a mysterious king.
The worship of others – was it that

Which gave me powers to heal, restore sight?
Speech, hearing, hearts?
It came from You, Father.

And is this really the end of all my glory?
The end of our time together, Me being here for You?
After all the followers, the friends… this?
Disappointing my brothers weighs heavy.
Unease with the deception I now represent.
I was supposed to be the Way and the Truth!
And this mangled mess of bones and blood – is this the Light?
Who will believe in me now,
Believe what I pronounced and promised?
I seem a fraud.

My own Father has let me die this way!
Nothing seems right about this.
Each moment I move up a bit
Carrying this load,
The nightmare feels impossible.
Is this real?
In this I know I am human.
It is far too much weight, too much bloodshed.
I feel that I cannot move up again.
A cruel whip provides assistance.

It was said of me
That I was sent by God.
That I was the favored One,
The promised Son.

Now this!

THE FIFTH SORROWFUL MYSTERY

THE CRUCIFIXION

Jesus Dies on the Cross

"Now from the sixth hour there was darkness over all the land until the ninth hour. And about the ninth hour Jesus cried with a loud voice ...'My God, my God, why have you forsaken me?'"
Matthew 27: 45-46

From the Tree of Life

The Crucifixion of Jesus

Thank You, Father
For not letting me go
Until I could make the arrangements
For my Mother Mary,

Until I could say goodbye
To my best friend, John.
Thank You, Father,
For completion in human terms.

And, my all-powerful Father,
Thank You for the little work detail
You gave me
To distract me from my own pain.

By Your grace I could converse with my neighbor
Revealing to him forgiveness
Offering him a place at my side
In paradise with Us.

That, my all-good Father,
Was grace — to continue my work
Until the very end.
So it could be a loving end
Not a bitter end.

My purpose driven life
Was this: to give to my neighbor
An invitation to heaven
Through contrition.

To heaven by acknowledgement,
To heaven by conversion of heart.

Father thank you
For letting me
Be Your Son,
Yourself in human form.

The nails in my hands,
And the nails piercing my feet
Were like axles
Holding this vehicle tied to the wood

Long enough to finish
Your work in me.
Gracious Father.
You sent enough of what I needed

To be hanging there –
My Mother, my best friend.
The neighbor recognizing You in me.
The rainstorm to wash over bloodied limbs.

Father,
You made it possible,
So my brothers and sisters remaining
Could know that nothing,

Nothing
Nothing
Is impossible
With You.

THE FIFTH SORROWFUL MYSTERY

THE CRUCIFIXION AS WITNESSED BY THE BLESSED VIRGIN MARY

The Pieta: Lowly the Light
Mary Remembers the Warning of the Prophet
Simeon: The Prophet's Words

"In him was life, and the life was the light of men. The light shines in the darkness, and the darkness has not overcome it." John 1: 4-5

Lowly the Light

Mary Beholds Her Son at Birth and at Death

Lowly the Light
Lay, flat
Atop a hill at the fall of dark.
The grisly grey-green clouds, like a waving drapery
Obscuring the view of the starlit universe.

Lowly laid, bare-bodied blood smudged
Mangled, bruised, and beat up as the
Fallen tree, His transport home.
Bowing low, my knees crunching
In the rocks, my lips approaching His stiff, still sacred face,
My breast joined to His own, bloodied Body.
Hearts merged,
Bodies attempted farewell.

Why did it feel like hello,
Bowing low to hover over You, Son?
To embrace You in the deep dark evening
When man fell, when God fell, was
A remembrance of the night we met
In an earthy manger, upon dew-dampened hay,
The animal stench drifting out disappearing.
It was the same moment, it was the same it was
Meeting my Lord-Son,
Bending low to adore You,

My lowly Light
Light of Life
Light of the world.

Lowly the Light came in the winter hay
Lowly the Light left, atop a dreadful hill, stretched in the soot.

At the first meeting, Light.
At time of farewell, Light.
My Child's body the vessel.
Two moments merge into one beginning
Recognizing my fugitive babe, and now
My crucified Lord, crushed and cast aside.

I surrender.

The Prophet's Words

Mary Knows the Sword Which Pierces Her Heart

knees buckled beneath me
my torso dropped down to the earth
warm liquid, wine colored, cushioned the fall.
the world seemed drowning in red.

my eyes blinked and closed
as I sank into a half sleep
with the heart of me tied, as it were
to an anchor.

there was a voice, a man's deep voice
calling to me from the past,
or from somewhere out in the universe,
calling to me in the dark abyss:

"A

Sword

Shall

Pierce

Your

Heart."

Suggestions for Reflection, Discussion, and Journaling

The First Sorrowful Mystery - The Agony in the Garden

"Lead, Blood, Mud"

1) At what time have I experienced dread in anticipation of the events I knew were to be taking place the next day?
   e.g. the night before a surgery, the funeral Mass for a loved one or the night before professional exams?

2) Recall the prayers you voiced to the Father.

The Second Sorrowful Mystery - The Scourging at the Pillar

"Cup of Lashes"

1) When a non-believing friend or colleague asks you why would God incarnate have to suffer torture this great, what do you tell him or her? Why would God allow His only Son, His favored One, to suffer this greatly?

2) Examining our behavior patterns, our habits of speech in interacting with others, and our attitudes toward others who are suffering, what is it that gives Jesus the most pain and sorrow?

3) What specifically must I do continually to reduce the hurt which I myself add to Jesus' suffering?

"Breaking Through Open Pores"

1) As we contemplate the sufferings of Jesus, we know that we desire to console Him in whatever way we are able. What are some of the things we can do to alleviate suffering around us?

2) Do you ever become involved in a cause that aims to console and assist those suffering in the world and then burn out on the effort? What causes this drop in our energy and what can we do about it?

3) What effect does the media and today's film industry have on our view of suffering and our reaction to it? Does exposure to the sight of torture and killing make people more violent? More indifferent?

4) Am I able to forgive and find compassion for individuals who have been guilty of violent crime? If I were asked to work with them, what influences might help?

5) Jesus' suffered the death penalty after accusations by members of his own community. Do you believe the death penalty serves as an effective tool for deterring violent crime, or is it societal revenge?

The Fourth Sorrowful Mystery - The Carrying of the Cross

"Nightmare Impossible"

1)   What are the crosses that God has asked me to carry in my past life? What were my sources of grace at those times?

2)   What crosses, burdens or problems beset me at this time?

3)   What response is the response that attracts grace for my soul with this particular cross?

4)   What is my program for fostering the state of grace in dealing with my current cross?

5)   What other sources of courage and fortitude could be out there for me?

6)   Knowing the pain Jesus carried when moving up to the appointed place for his death, how do I, like Veronica or Simon, make effort to lift our Lord's burden?

7)   When I must pay in some way for the sins of others, am I able to become closer to Jesus, rather than react in anger?

The Fifth Sorrowful Mystery - The Crucifixion

"From the Tree of Life"

1)   When I must suffer extreme pain, do I go to Jesus for example?

2)   What does Jesus do during the time He endures the worst possible pain?

3) Do I strive to reach out and console others, share, care and lend hope when I am in pain and turmoil?

4) In times of pain, do I receive grace by caring for someone else, who has perhaps received less in the course of life?

"The Prophet's Words"

1) What would you consider the "worst possible pain?" e.g. loss of spouse, loss of a child?

2) How do I prepare for such a trial or cross?

3) Do I make a practice of assisting those in suffering?

"Lowly the Light"

1) Recall 2-3 times in your life when God's powerful love was shown to you and you felt it unmistakably.

2) Call to mind a time in your life of devastation, tragedy, loss, or sorrow when you encountered God in a totally different way. What channels of grace do you remember?

3) Do I reach upward regularly to receive special graces? How? What additional discipline could help?

Being There At The Scene Of

The Glorious Mysteries

THE FIRST GLORIOUS MYSTERY

THE RESURRECTION

Jesus is Risen From the Dead

"Why do you seek the living among the dead? He is not here, but has risen! Luke 24: 5

Preparing the Miracle of the Rising

The Resurrection of our Lord
as Told by the Angels who Prepared His Sacred Body

Our Commander, the King of Kings, the Lord of Lords,
Summoned the two of us. We were
Two trusted angels chosen from legions of others
Who filled the heavens.

Our Lord, Brother Jesus, lay peaceful but cold
In the sparse stone room
Wrapped in lily white linens
His royal visage tilted to the side.

Jesus shared the journey of mortal men
Even to the tomb.

We heard the voice of the Father, clear and strong –
Commanding us attend His Son now
And prepare His body for the miracle of His rising.
Instantly we were inside the stone walls with our Master.

We had ministered to His precious body before.
After His mortification in the desert.
We were our Lord's nurse angels.
What glorious privilege we shared!

The powerful fragrance of myrrh
Surrounding Him there,
And the secret excitement of the miracle to come
Made our work delightful.

We brought with us healing balms
From heaven's pharmacy – Eden's herbs, fruits, and extracts.
Heaven's nurses came prepared!
Cautiously our hands approached His sacred head.
We went to work in grace, removing the thorns one by one
Then dressing the wounds.
Infinite love poured through our hands,
The Love of God's own heart,
Gentle to heal, powerful to restore His blessed flesh.

In middle of night, when at last our work was done
Two powerful archangels arrived
To move the stone from the entrance to the tomb.
The two of us were returned to rejoin our ranks
And await the miracle of the morning when the light would rise.

THE SECOND GLORIOUS MYSTERY

THE ASCENSION

Jesus is Taken into Heaven

"Then he led them out as far as Bethany, and lifting up his hands he blessed them. While he blessed them, he parted from them, and was carried up into heaven." Luke 24: 50-51

Charging for Departure

The Ascension of our Lord

As much as the need to come is this need to depart.
My work with you, my friends
Changes.

What appears to be my body rises
As I make my final promises
To stay with you always.

Even as I lift, radiant in victory
The breeze beneath me turns to wind and fire
Of the Spirit in you.

It is time. In you, my disciples
I know my Father's work will be complete
To gather in all the nations.

As the clouds become a haphazard staircase
I send you my Truth, my Peace, my Love, my Promise.
I ascend joyfully into the atmosphere beyond the veil of the known.

The wings of destiny stretch stable beneath me
As my settled soul assumes its rightful place
In the universe. A niche I know – Beloved Son. I return home.

You shed tears, lean on one another.
You must dance. My work will charge forth in you
Until the very end of time.

THE THIRD GLORIOUS MYSTERY

THE DESCENT OF THE HOLY SPIRIT UPON THE APOSTLES

The Holy Spirit Descends in Tongues of Fire

"And there appeared to them tongues as of fire, distributed and resting on each one of them. And they were all filled with the Holy Spirit and began to speak in other tongues, as the Spirit gave them utterance." Acts 2: 3-4

Fountains of Fire

The Descent of the Holy Spirit Upon the Apostles

Fountains of fire
Flowed out upon us – a
Wondrous fireball of truth

Splintering into dancing tongues
Sent to dazzle each one of us
Burning into us new selves!

In our upper room,
As the fire fell, our hearts beat faster
In frightened awe.

Our lips began to move furiously!
And unintentionally, there came a spontaneous
Combustion of joyful praise!

All the languages of the world
Converged like rivers joining in profusion.
It was a confluence of ecstasies!

Hearts, continents, cultures
Channeled back to the creation of man
Adam found his new voice here in the Upper Room.

Whispering, murmuring, shouting an answer
To the Maker in effervescent praise.
The tribes of man responded to the Creator's mighty voice

With a "Yes!" to overflow to the ends of the earth
To light and fire the face of the planet
In unison praising the Master Mind of creation

Who danced down
In tongues of fire
That day.

THE FOURTH GLORIOUS MYSTERY

THE ASSUMPTION OF MARY

The Blessed Virgin Mary Ascends into Heaven

Our Mother is Taken to Heaven

The Assumption of Mary Told by a Nurse Tending the Aged Virgin

Not long after her beloved Son
Had made His last appearance,
Leaving us with a promise,
We began to look after His Mother.

John, His beloved disciple, took seriously
The pledge he gave at the foot of the cross.
And we, the women of the city of Ephesus
Lovingly joined in.

She was like love itself – that makes all things simple.
Easy to serve, her natural spirit of sweetness
Flowed from her. She belonged to us –
The families of Ephesus.

I was a servant to her.
Our Mother Mary had advanced in years.
What a thrill it was
To care for her as a daughter would.

I had been appointed and anointed for the mission!
The honor had quieted my noise and love for chatter.
Our Mother needed me!
My community needed me.

Each week, we would accompany her
To the center of town where the Scriptures were read.

Before too long a time had passed
We began to carry our Mother there in a cart which we
Fixed with linens and mounds of fabric
For her safety and comfort.

For Mary, Sabbath prayer gave meaning,
The reason for life itself.

Then her time came.
She needed to stay home that fateful week.
So unlike Mother. Our Mother
Who kept many things inside her heart.

It was I who stayed back to tend her every need.
For me, to be near her was like sacred time in synagogue.
Only sweeter, quieter –
Infinitely sweet, infinitely warm.

That bright and memorable morn, she signaled to me of her need
To step outdoors in the sun, to greet her God.
It may have been that special spot
In the history of man, where the angel first came to her.

I gave her time.

A little while and I went out.
What I beheld would be history!
A courtyard radiant with light beams like a transfiguration –
Powerful to behold, difficult to imagine.

Mary our Mother had been taken.
The others from Temple arrived in time and brought whole families.
Mary's courtyard of light became a little temple
Of mystery and love and the destiny of man.

THE FIFTH GLORIOUS MYSTERY

THE CORONATION OF THE BLESSED MOTHER IN HEAVEN

Mother Mary is Crowned Queen of Heaven

"And a great sign appeared in heaven, a woman clothed with the sun, with the moon under her feet, and on her head a crown of twelve stars..." Revelation 12:1

The Revelation Comes Alive

The Crowning of the Queen Mother Today and Always

It goes on each evening of the calendar year – her crowning ceremony.
In Lourdes, where healing waters gush freely from the mountainside
And the waters of the Gave River cuddle thousands of pilgrims,
The Spirit of Mary fills the air.
Pilgrims come from every nation, every day of the year
To breathe in her motherly love, to bathe in the waters
Which confer her loving touch, to taste the sweetness of her heart.
Many are called, but few are chosen.

Each evening her children process in with their candles lit
Their hearts in love, coming to praise her,
Sing for her, be with her, crown her.
Coming to her sanctuary, the pilgrim feels a home
And her children come in droves from every land and nation.
They come in native dress of many cultures –
The dark ones, the light ones, the babes,
The young couples, the aged, those on stretchers needing relief.

They join in the marvelous chorus, sung around the world –
"Immaculate Mary, Thy praises we sing!"
The confluent harmony of many tongues
Fills this throng and joins them as one.

The great sign which appeared in the sky
Is revealed before the eye.
In Lourdes, the woman clothed with the sun lives,
Breathes, enwraps us in the here and now.

The revelation comes alive.

Suggestions for Reflection, Discussion, and Journaling

The First Glorious Mystery - The Resurrection of the Lord Jesus

"Preparing the Miracle of the Rising"

1) Do you find the teaching of the bodily Resurrection of Jesus to be a difficult one? Why or why not?

2) Do you believe those who testify that Jesus has appeared to them, and that they met with Him in this vision?

3) What is the definition of a miracle? What are a few miracles which have occurred in recent times? Have you had a hard time believing in them?

4) Do you pray to a particular saint for miracles you hope for? How did you become aware of his or her intercessory power?

The Second Glorious Mystery - The Ascension of the Lord

"Charging for Departure"

1) At the scene of His Ascension into heaven, Jesus promised that He would be with us until the end of time. Make a list of the times in your life when Jesus was most evidently present right alongside you.

2) Have you ever testified to this feeling, either in private or in public? Why or why not? To whom?

3) What are some of the clearest signs of Christ's ongoing presence in our community and our world?

4) Does my daily life reflect the living Christ still among us?
How? Who are the people most influenced by my actions in witness of Christ's Word among us?

5) What are a few specific ways in which I could become a more powerful witness to Christ's life among us currently?

The Third Glorious Mystery - The Descent of the Holy Spirit upon the Apostles

"Fountains of Fire"

1) Where do you see the Holy Spirit descending upon us regularly in today's world?

2) Describe to a non-believer, the action of the Holy Spirit in your heart which takes place at Mass, or during certain types of prayer services.

3) Describe to a non-believer the action of the Holy Spirit as a result of family prayer time. What happens during personal time spent in the Scriptures?

4) What are a few clear signs that the Holy Spirit is alive and active in a Church community?

5) Have you experienced Charismatic prayer?

6) If yes, what was your reaction?

The Fourth Glorious Mystery - The Assumption of the Blessed Virgin Mary

"Our Mother is Taken to Heaven"

1) Do you find the teaching of the Assumption of the Blessed Virgin Mary to be a difficult one to accept? Why or why not?

2) When you imagine the scene of the Assumption, do you imagine others present? If so, who would be there? Make an effort to assemble the members of the Holy Family's extended family who may still be present nearby.

The Fifth Glorious Mystery - The Coronation of the Blessed Mother

"The Revelation Comes Alive"

1) Consider yourself invited to the Coronation of the Blessed Mother. What would you wish to bring as your special gift to her on this occasion?

2) In prayer time, consider what new habit or attitude you could adopt which would make your Mother in Heaven the most happy.

3) Imagine yourself approaching the Blessed Mother in person after she has been crowned. Allow yourself to accept her motherly love for you.

4) Imagine that the Blessed Mother asks you how she can help you. You go home and write her a letter.

How to Say the Rosary

To enter into your prayer space, hold the Crucifix attached to the Rosary, and make the **Sign of the Cross**, saying: "In the Name of the Father, and of the Son, and of the Holy Spirit, Amen." Then, recite **The Apostles Creed** or **The Nicene Creed**: "I believe in God, the Father Almighty, Creator of heaven and earth. And in Jesus Christ, His only Son, our Lord, who was crucified, died and was buried. He descended into hell. On the third day He rose again from the dead. He is seated at the right hand of God the Father Almighty. From where He will come to judge the living and the dead. I believe in the Holy Spirit, the Holy Catholic Church, the forgiveness of sins, the resurrection of the body, and life everlasting. Amen." (The Apostles Creed)

Move to the first bead. Say the **Our Father**: "Our Father, Who art in heaven, hallowed be Thy Name. Thy kingdom come, Thy Will be done, on earth as it is in heaven. Give us this day our daily bread, and forgive us our trespasses as we forgive those who trespass against us, and deliver us from evil. Amen."

On the next three beads, say the **Hail Mary**: "Hail, Mary, full of grace, the Lord is with thee. Blessed art thou among women, and blessed is the fruit of thy womb. Holy Mary, Mother of God, pray for us now, and at the hour of our death. Amen."

On the last bead of the Introductory Prayers say the **Glory Be**: "Glory be to the Father, and to the Son and to the Holy Spirit. As it was in the beginning, is now, and ever shall be world without end. Amen."

Now enter into **The Mysteries of the Rosary.**

There are five sets of ten (10) beads. Each set of 10 beads is referred to as "a decade" of the Rosary. First, the leader announces the Mystery of the Rosary, which is meditated upon during recitation of the Our Father and the ten Hail Mary's of this set of prayers. If an individual is praying the Rosary in private, he or she will say in silence what the leader would say in public: e.g. "The First Joyful Mystery, The Annunciation." The individual, in prayer, sets their mind upon this event or scene, and meditates upon it while reciting the following prayers:

The **Our Father** is said, holding the Rosary section of tiny rope before this decade (10 beads).

The ten (10) **Hail Mary's** are now recited silently or out loud in the case of a group praying together.

The **Glory Be** is then said, concluding the recitation of the First Mystery.

The leader, or the individual praying privately, then announces the Second Mystery, e.g. "The Second Joyful Mystery, The Visitation."

The Our Father.
The ten (10) Hail Mary's.
 The Glory Be.

(All said while reflecting on the Visitation, or the Second Mystery.)

The leader, or the individual in prayer then announces the Third Mystery, e.g. "The Third Joyful Mystery, The Birth of our Lord."

The Our Father.
The ten (10) Hail Mary's.
The Glory Be.

The leader or the individual then announces the Fourth Mystery, e.g. "The Fourth Joyful Mystery, the Presentation in the Temple."

The Our Father.
The ten (10) Hail Mary's.
The Glory Be.

The leader or the individual then announces the Fifth Mystery, e.g. "The Fifth Joyful Mystery, The Finding of the Child Jesus in the Temple."

The Our Father.
The ten (10) Hail Mary's.
The Glory Be.

The five (5) decades of the Rosary are now concluded.

Most often the Rosary is officially concluded with **The Memorare**, and/or a few other special prayers in which we invoke the intercession of our Lady.

The Memorare

"Remember O most gracious Virgin Mary, that never was it known that anyone who fled to thy protection, implored Thy help, or sought Thy intercession was left unaided. Inspired by this confidence, I fly unto Thee, O Virgin of Virgins my Mother. To thee I come, before thee I stand, sinful and sorrowful. Oh Mother of the Word Incarnate, despise not my petitions, but hear and answer me. Amen."

Mysteries of the Rosary for Each Day of the Week

Monday: The Joyful Mysteries

Tuesday: The Sorrowful Mysteries

Wednesday: The Glorious Mysteries

Thursday: The Luminous Mysteries

Friday: The Sorrowful Mysteries

Saturday: The Joyful Mysteries

Sunday: Variable according to the liturgical season.

Suggested Reading

For Biblical Texts

The Ignatius Catholic Study Bible: The New Testament. Revised Standard Version Second Catholic Edition. With Introduction, Commentary, and Notes by Scott Hahn and Curtis Mitch. Ignatius Press, San Francisco, 2010.

Lincoln McVeigh, Poetry from the Bible. New York: Dial Press, 1925.

For Marian Art and Poetry in History

Lawrence Cunningham and Nicolas Sapieha, Mother of God. San Francisco, Harper and Row Publishers, 1982. The Preface by Mary Gordon thoughtfully examines and underscores how it is though poetry, painting, sculpture and music that one finds a sure connection to the Mother of God.

Linda Ching Sledge, Shivering Babe, Victorious Lord: The Nativity in Poetry and Art, Grand Rapids, Michigan, William B. Eerdmans Publishing Company, 1981. A comprehensive study of Mary in Art and Poetry from the 14th Century to Modern Times

For Spiritual Poetry

Pope John Paul II, <u>The Poetry of John Paul II,</u> Translated by Jerzy Peterkiewicz. Washington, D.C., United States Conference of Catholic Bishops Publishing, 2003.

Alan Jacobs, editor, <u>Poetry for the Spirit.</u> New York, Barnes and Noble, 2002. This anthology of spiritual poetry is a revised edition of <u>The Elemental Book of Spiritual Verse.</u>

W.H. Gardner and N.H. MacKenzie, editors, <u>The Poems of Gerard Manley Hopkins.</u> New York, Oxford University Press, 1970. The Jesuit poet's rendering of "The Virgin Mary as Compared to the Air We Breathe" is a potentially life-altering experience of Mary's ubiquitous presence with us suffusing our surroundings in the natural world.

Constance and Daniel Pollock, Editors, <u>Visions of the Afterlife, Heaven, Hell and Revelation as Viewed by</u> the World's Great Writers. Nashville, Tennessee, Word Publishing, 1999. A compilation of poetry and prose from Emily Dickinson, John Donne, Alfred Lord Tennyson, Charles Dickens, C.S. Lewis, Christina Rosseti and other classic writers.

Joyce Kilmer, editor, <u>Dreams and Images: An Anthology of Catholic Poets</u>. New York, Boni and Liveright, 1917.

For Mystical Spirituality

<u>Patricia Hampl, editor, Teresa of Avila: Selections from The Interior Castle</u>. San Francisco, Harper San Francisco, 2004.

St. Therese of Lisieux, <u>Story of a Soul: The Autobiography of St. Therese of Lisieux.</u> Washington, D.C., ICS Publications, 1976.

Cindy Cavner, editor, <u>Prayers and Meditations of Therese of Lisieux</u>. Ann Arbor, Michigan, Servant Publications, 1992.

Brother Lawrence, <u>The Practice of the Presence of God, with Spiritual Maxims</u>. Grand Rapids, J, Spire Books, 1967.

For Prayer and the Spiritual Journey

Anthony Mottola, <u>The Spiritual Exercises of St. Ignatius.</u> Garden City, Doubleday, 1964.

John Olin, editor, <u>The Autobiography of St. Ignatius Loyola, with Related Documents</u>. New York, Fordham University Press, 1992.

Mother Teresa of Calcutta, <u>No Greater Love.</u> Edited by Becky Benenate and Joseph Durepos, with a Foreword by Thomas Moore. Novato, California, New World Library, 1997.

Robert Waldron, <u>Walking with Henri Nouwen, A Reflective Journey.</u> New York, Paulist Press, 2003.

Rich Cleveland, <u>The Seven Last Words of Christ: A Bible Study of Jesus' Passion</u>. Ijamsville, Maryland, The Word Among Us Press, 2002. An in-depth study of Jesus' last words with suggestions for personal reflection.

Robert Ignatius Guste, <u>Mary at my Side.</u> Santa Barbara, California, Queenship Publishing Company, 1993. Fr. Guste shares his personal journey with Mary as His companion.

Thomas H. Green, S.J. <u>A Vacation with the Lord, A Personal Directed Retreat.</u> Notre Dame, Indiana, Ave Maria Press, 1986.

Immaculee Ilibigaza, <u>Left to Tell: Discovering God Amidst the Rwandan Holocaust.</u> Carlsbad, California, Hay House, Inc., 2006. One of the most renowned public speakers in the world, Immaculee tells her gripping story of surviving torturous captivity witnessing grotesque atrocities through the continuous use of Our Lady's Rosary, the one possession she had with her when she became imprisoned.

Michael Casey, <u>Sacred Reading: The Ancient Art of Lectio Divina.</u> Liquori, Missouri, Triumph Books, 1996.

Lyn Holley Doucet and Robin Hebert, <u>When Wisdom Speaks: Living Experiences of Biblical Women.</u> New York, The Crossroad Publishing Company, 2007. Two Teresian laywomen prayerfully share stories of personal transformation through entering into the experiences of Biblical women.

For Study of Jesus' Roots in Jewish Culture

Brant Pitre, <u>Jesus and the Jewish Roots of the Eucharist: Unlocking the Secrets of the Last Supper.</u> New York, Doubleday, 2011. World-renowned scholar Dr. Brant Pitre situates the institution of the Eucharistic Liturgy as it emerges from and revolutionizes the Jewish Passover.

Photo Credits

COVER PHOTO:

1. Carl Heinrich Bloch (1834-1890) Danish
   "The Annunciation" Oil on Copper Plate
   Photo Credit: The Hope Gallery

INTERIOR PHOTOS:

2. Michelangelo Merisi da Caravaggio (1571-1610) Italian
   "The Annunciation" 1608, Oil on Canvas
   Current Location: Musee des Beaux-Arts de Nancy, Nancy
   Photo Credit: Copyright: Public Domain in the United
   States. Source: Wikimedia.org

3. Rembrandt Harmensz van Rijn (1606-1669) Dutch
   "The Adoration of the Shepherds" 1646, Oil on Canvas,
   Style: Baroque
   Current Location: National Gallery, London, Great Britain
   Photo Credit, Copyright: National Gallery, London/Art
   Resource, NY

4. Rembrandt Harmensz van Rijn (1606-1669) Dutch
   "Presentation in the Temple (Simeon)" 1669, Oil on Canvas
   Current Location: National Museum, Stockholm, Sweden
   Photo Credit: Kavalier/ Art Resource, NY

5. Carl Heinrich Bloch (1834-1890) Danish
   "Gethsemane (Study)" Oil on Canvas
   Photo Credit: The Hope Gallery

6. Michelangelo Merisi da Caravaggio (1571-1610) Italian
   "The Crowning with Thorns" 1602-1604, Oil on Canvas
   Current Location: Kunsthistorisches Museum, Vienna
   Photo Credit, Copyright: Public Domain in the United
   States, Google art project, Source Wikimedia.org

7. Rembrandt Harmensz van Rijn (1606-1669) Dutch
   "Descent from the Cross" 1634
   Current Location: Hermitage Museum, Saint Petersburg,
   Russia
   Photo Credit: Photos.com, Copyright: Getty Images

8. Paolo Veronese (1528-1588) Italian
   "Pieta" 1581, Oil on Canvas
   Current Location: Hermitage Museum, Saint Petersburg,
   Russia
   Photo Credit: Jupiter Images, Copyright: Getty Images

9. Carl Heinrich Bloch (1834-1890) Danish
   "Resurrection (Altarpiece)" Oil on Canvas
   Photo Credit: The Hope Gallery

10. "Flemish School, 16th Century Christianity"
    Photo Credit: Photos.com, Copyright: Getty Images

11. Bartolome Esteban Murillo (1617-1682) Spanish
    "Immaculate Conception"
    Photo Credit: Photos.com, Copyright: Getty Images

12. "The Assumption of the Virgin", Painting by Lefasse
Photo Credit: Photos.com, Copyright: Getty Images

13. Carl Heinrich Bloch (1834-1890) Danish
"The Baptism" Oil on Copper Plate
Photo Credit: The Hope Gallery

14. Carl Heinrich Bloch (1834-1890) Danish
"Transfiguration of Christ" Oil on Copper Plate
Photo Credit: The Hope Gallery

15. Carl Heinrich Bloch (1834-1890) Danish
"The Last Supper" Oil on Copper Plate
Photo Credit: The Hope Gallery